A WINNING SKILLS BOOK

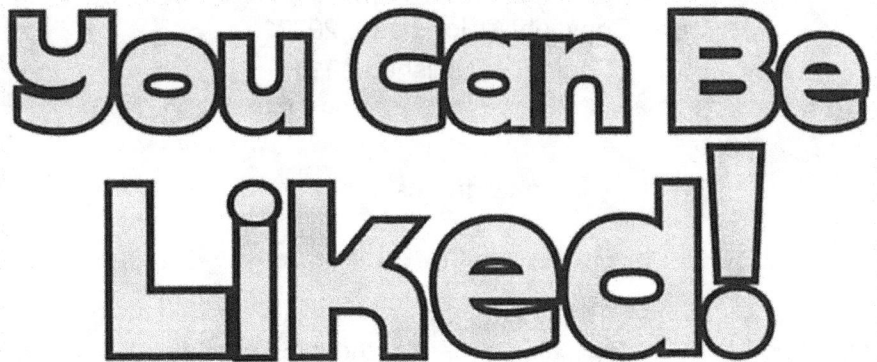

Joy Berry

Illustrated by Bartholomew

Joy Berry Enterprises

Copyright © Joy Berry, 2022
Originally Published 2013

All rights are reserved.

No part of this book can be duplicated or used without the prior written permission of the copyright owner, except for the use of brief quotations from the book.

For inquiries or permission requests contact the publisher.

Published by Joy Berry Enterprises
www.joyberryenterprises.com

Joy Berry Enterprises

You can be liked if you know about
- physical and social needs
- eight social needs
- the importance of contributing to others
- fulfilling other people's social needs, and
- the right attitudes.

INTRODUCTION

INTRODUCTION   5

"YOU DON'T HAVE TO BE STRANDED ON AN ISLAND TO BE LONELY. JUST THINK ABOUT SOME OF THE KIDS AT SCHOOL WHO DON'T HAVE FRIENDS."

"I CAN RELATE! I FIND IT EXTREMELY **DIFFICULT** TO MAKE NEW FRIENDS! I KEEP THINKING THERE'S GOT TO BE A TRICK TO IT!"

"YEAH, I GUESS IT'S HARD FOR SOME KIDS TO MAKE FRIENDS."

"HUMPH! TRY BEING A BUG! EVERYONE TRIES TO SHOO YOU AWAY! **SIGH!**"

PHYSICAL AND SOCIAL NEEDS

Your body needs certain things in order to survive and grow. These needs are called **physical needs.**

Just as you have physical needs, you have **social needs.**

PHYSICAL AND SOCIAL NEEDS 7

You need other people. You depend on them to give you the things you cannot give yourself. The things you need from other people are called **social needs.** Eight of them are listed and explained on the next few pages.

Social Need #1: You Need Attention

You need to have other people pay attention to you. You need to be noticed in a positive way.

When people notice you, you feel important. Feeling important can help you value yourself and motivate you to take good care of yourself.

Social Need #2: You Need Acceptance

You need to have other people accept you. You need to have them let you know that you are OK.

When people feel good about you, you feel good about yourself. Feeling good about yourself can help you become a happier, healthier person.

Social Need #3: You Need Appreciation

You need to have people appreciate your good qualities. You also need to have them appreciate your accomplishments.

Appreciation can make you want to continue being a good person and doing positive things. This can help you become a better person.

Social Need #4: You Need Encouragement

It is important for you to feel that you can succeed. You need to have other people encourage you when you try to do something. You also need encouragement when you make a mistake or fail.

The assurance you receive from others can give you the confidence to keep trying. This confidence to keep trying is important because you cannot achieve anything unless you try.

Social Need #5: You Need Help

Sometimes there are things that you cannot do by yourself. You need to have other people help you.

It is good to accept help from others. Their assistance can enable you to accomplish much more than you could do by yourself.

Social Need #6: You Need Fellowship

Fellowship is spending time with other people and sharing your good and bad experiences with them.

It is easier for you to handle the bad things that happen to you if you share them with other people. If you share your good times with others, you can enjoy those good times more. Sharing your experiences can enhance the quality of your life.

Social Need #7: You Need Equal Treatment

You need to have other people be fair with you. You need to have them give to you as much as you give to them.

If people take more from you than they give, you may become resentful. Resentment can cause you to be very unhappy.

Social Need #8: You Need Resolution

Resolution is solving a difficulty that you have with another person. When people have done something wrong to you or have hurt you, you might feel bad. You need to resolve the difficulty so that you can feel good again. You need to know that the people who hurt you are sorry for what they have done. You also need to know that they are doing their best to rectify their wrongdoing.

If people who have wronged you do not respond this way, you might develop hostile feelings about them. These feelings can cause you to be very unhappy.

You need:
- Attention
- Acceptance
- Appreciation
- Encouragement
- Help
- Fellowship
- Equal treatment
- Resolution

You cannot give these things to yourself. You must receive them from other people. Other people are usually willing to give you what you need if they like you. This is why it is important to be liked by others.

You can encourage other people to like you by treating them the way you want to be treated. Other people have the same social needs that you have. If you want them to fulfill your needs you must try to fulfill theirs.

THE IMPORTANCE OF CONTRIBUTING TO OTHERS

Three very important things can happen when you fulfill other people's social needs.
1. You will feel good about doing something good for others.
2. The people you help will need you.
3. The people you help will like you.

When other people need you and like you, they give you what you need in exchange for your giving them what they need.

Therefore, having your own social needs met begins with your contributing to the social needs of other people.

The next few pages will tell you how to respond to other people's needs.

FULFILLING OTHER PEOPLE'S SOCIAL NEEDS

Other People Need Attention

Talking with other people is one way to give them attention. Most people respond well if you
- talk about them in a positive way,
- talk about the people, places, and things that interest them, and
- refer to them by name when you talk to them.

Listening to others is another way to give them attention. People know that you are listening to them if you
- look into their eyes while they are talking,
- do not interrupt them, and
- let them know that you are interested in what they are saying.

Other People Need Acceptance

Accepting people is believing that they are OK the way they are. Most people feel accepted if you
- value them (realize they are important),
- treat them with kindness and respect, and
- tell them you think they are OK.

FULFILLING OTHER PEOPLE'S SOCIAL NEEDS

When you accept other people, you do not try to change them. This means that you
- try not to judge others (do not decide whether they are right or wrong),
- try not to nag others (do not constantly complain to them about their faults), and
- focus on the good qualities rather than the bad qualities of others.

Other People Need Appreciation

You can find good qualities in every person. People need to have these good qualities appreciated. They will know you appreciate them if you
- tell them what you think are their good qualities,
- tell them why you think these good qualities are important, and
- encourage them to develop their good qualities and to share them with others.

FULFILLING OTHER PEOPLE'S SOCIAL NEEDS

People need to be appreciated for the good things they do for you. They will know you appreciate them if you
- thank them for whatever they have done,
- do whatever you can to show your appreciation, and
- offer to return the favor.

Other People Need Encouragement

People need to be encouraged to try. You can encourage them if you
- let them know you are confident they can do what they are trying to do,
- recognize and congratulate them for any progress they make, and
- help them in any way you can.

FULFILLING OTHER PEOPLE'S SOCIAL NEEDS

People need to be encouraged when they make a mistake or fail. You can help them if you
- remind them that no one is perfect and that everyone makes mistakes,
- tell them about some of your mistakes and how you survived them, and
- assure them they can learn from their mistakes and become better people.

Other People Need Help

People may need you to help them when they have problems. They will welcome your assistance if you

- try to put yourself in their place and understand what they are going through,
- let them decide how much or how little they tell you about their problems, and
- try not to criticize them or offer advice unless they ask you to.

You may need to help other people.
- Offer you assistance whenever you can. (Make sure you are able to follow through with any promises you make.)
- Try not to take over or become bossy. (Do only what the other people want you to do.)
- Work hard and do your best when you do something for others.

Other People Need Fellowship

When good things happen to other people they may want to share their happiness with you.

- Be happy for them and let them know you share in their happiness.
- Try not to be jealous.
- Remember that good things have happened and will continue to happen to you, too.

FULFILLING OTHER PEOPLE'S SOCIAL NEEDS

People may also want to share their difficult experiences with you.
- Remember that it usually takes a long time for people to get over a difficult experience. Let them talk to you about it as much as they need to do so.
- Tell them about some of your bad experiences and how you survived them.
- Assure them that, like all difficult experiences, this one will pass and something good will take its place.

Other People Need Equal Treatment

Most people want to be fair with you. You can help them be fair if you
- make sure they are aware of what you are doing for them,
- let them know what they can do for you in return if they should offer, and
- graciously accept whatever they do for you.

People need to be treated fairly. You can be fair if you
- try to be aware of the other things people do for you,
- find out what they want in return, and
- do your best to contribute what they want.

Other People Need Resolution

People need to know that you are sorry when you have done something wrong to them. They will know you are sorry if you
- admit that you have done something wrong,
- say that you are sorry,
- do everything you can to make up for the wrongdoing (make sure that your efforts are acceptable to the other people), and
- try not to do the same thing again.

People need you forgiveness when they have done something wrong to you. They will know that they are forgiven when you
- accept their apology,
- help them decide what they can do to make up for their wrongdoing,
- accept whatever they do to show you that they are sorry, and
- try to forget what they did and do not keep bringing it up to them.

FULFILLING OTHER PEOPLE'S SOCIAL NEEDS

Like you, other people have social needs.

They need:
- Attention
- Acceptance
- Appreciation
- Encouragement
- Help
- Fellowship
- Equal treatment
- Resolution

There are people around you who need others to help fulfill their social needs. These people can become your friends.

THE RIGHT ATTITUDE

The things that you do for other people must be done with the right attitude. The right attitude comes from knowing that
- other people are special, and
- other people are valuable.

When you think of other people in this way, you care for them. Caring is the attitude that makes you **want** to give other people the things they need. Your wanting to meet other people's needs makes them more receptive to your efforts, and this makes your efforts more effective.

CONCLUSION

You can be liked if you care for other people and treat them the way you want to be treated.